Learning & Growing Together

Learning and growing together is like dancing. Step by step, day by day, you and your child learn about each other and how your relationship works. Sometimes you lead, and sometimes you follow your child in the dance you create together.

ZERO TO THREE®

This guide is for you—mothers, fathers, and others who have primary responsibility for raising a baby or toddler. You are the most important people in your child's life. In the coming pages, we will help you discover that you are your own best resource for understanding and caring for your young child.

"Yeah, right!" you may think. You are recalling a time when you tried unsuccessfully to calm your screaming baby. Or the time you stood in the supermarket aisle, embarrassed and frustrated, because your toddler planted herself on the floor at your feet and refused to budge. You're not alone. These things happen in the lives of most parents.

Parenting is a lifelong learning process, and no one has all of the answers. Hitting on the right solution is a matter of trial and error. And even when you do all of the "right" things, your child may not respond the way you thought she would. It often seems that by the time you figure out a good way to handle something, you're on to yet another challenge.

In the pages that follow, we provide information and tools to help you build a strong foundation for your child's development. Our focus is on you, your child, and the dance that is your everyday life together. With this solid base, you can go on to read about specific child-rearing topics like sleep, toilet teaching, or sibling rivalry, and decide what makes sense for you, your child, and your family.

Parenting is a lifelong learning process,
and no one has all of the answers.

1 How Parenthood Feels

THINK ABOUT WHO YOU ARE AS A PARENT BY LOOKING AT:

- the profound impact becoming a parent has on your life
- how your own life experiences influence the kind of parent you become
- the importance of taking time for yourself and for the critical relationships in your life

2 Tuning In to Your Child

DISCOVER WHO YOUR CHILD IS AND HOW YOU CAN BEST NURTURE HER TALENTS BY EXPLORING:

- how she learns about the world through her senses (seeing, hearing, tasting, smelling, and touching)
- her personal style
- five traits of temperament
- parenting strategies to match your child's individual needs

3 The Amazing First Three Years of Life

COME TO UNDERSTAND:

- how babies and toddlers think and feel
- how babies and toddlers learn
- the basics on brain development
- typical child behaviors, what they might mean, and how you can respond in a helpful way

4 In Conclusion: Thoughts to Grow On

Think about some questions to help you tune in to how you and your child learn and grow together every day.

Note: Throughout this guide, we use he and she
interchangeably to refer to babies and toddlers.

1. How Parenthood *Feels*

WHO AM I?

Because you are the most important person in your child's life, we begin with you. Like all parents, you want to do the best job possible raising your child. To achieve this goal, there is probably no single quality more important than self-awareness. The better you understand why you do what you do, the better equipped you'll be to make good decisions and to rethink your decisions when things don't work out the way you wanted. Parents need to be flexible, and self-awareness is the key to flexibility. Ultimately, your self-awareness will promote your child's development, as well as help the two of you develop a satisfying and loving relationship.

But developing self-awareness isn't easy. It requires thinking about how your life experiences, along with your hopes and expectations, shape the kind of parent you will become. Remember—your child does not need you to be a super parent. What she does need are parents who are willing to understand, accept, and appreciate her for who she is. And you can't really do that until you know yourself. Once you understand who you are, you can begin to understand how you are similar and different from your child and separate your needs from hers.

Let's look at how one parent, Marie, uses what she knows about herself to work out a challenging situation with her toddler:

One morning Marie's 2 1/2-year-old daughter, Kayla, pulls open the drawer of her dresser and announces, "I want flower shirt." As she peers into another drawer, she says, "I want this pants...and this," holding up a pair of blue and red striped pants and a neon green skirt. Marie has to hold herself back. Not only is it a ghastly combination, but truth be told, she's worried what people will think if Kayla wanders out of the house in that get-up.

It's a terrible time for a battle. Marie is already behind schedule and can't risk being late for work. On the other hand, she can hear her own mother's voice, cautioning, "Who's running your family? If you let Kayla make the

Do you think you were prepared for parenthood?

What was your biggest surprise?

What was your biggest disappointment?

How often do you stop to think about why you do what you do as a parent?

Thinking about your reactions to your child enables you to reconsider your actions and make new choices.

decisions, she'll end up being spoiled. Children need to know who's boss!"

Marie feels her stomach tightening. She doesn't want Kayla to feel what she felt growing up—resentment at not being able to make any decisions for herself. In fact, she's impressed by her daughter's assertiveness and admires the fact that she seems to know what she wants and feels strongly enough to ask for it.

Marie takes everything into consideration and decides on a compromise. She lets Kayla choose what to wear, but with certain limits. She can't wear a skirt *and* pants at the same time, but she can wear whatever color combinations she chooses. As Kayla prances out the door in her neon shirt and striped pants, Marie is able to laugh and say, "You look as bright as the sunshine, Kayla!"

The process of thinking through her initial reaction makes Marie her own best resource. Her compromise took into account her personal values—wanting Kayla to look presentable—and respect for her daughter's independent thinking. Marie knows that she and her daughter are two separate people. There will probably be lots of things they'll disagree on in the years ahead, but Marie's self-awareness will help them problem-solve together and build a loving relationship.

How Your Childhood Experiences Influence the Way You Parent

Many of your beliefs, attitudes, and expectations were molded during your childhood, and all of them influence your parenting style. Tuning in, as Marie did, to the ways in which your own childhood experiences shape the kind of parent you become can be difficult. If you grew up in a supportive, nurturing family, you will have learned many positive lessons about parenting. But people who grew up in less than perfect environments—in homes where there was conflict, neglect, violence, health problems, or substance abuse—are by no means destined to replay their own parents' mistakes. In fact, they often create exactly the kind of nurturing, loving family they were denied as children. The key is to be aware of your own feelings about parenthood and understand the motivations for your actions.

Let's look at how two parents, based on their perspectives and beliefs, react differently to the issue of their baby's independence:

When 6-month-old Lexi cries, her mom, Sandra, waits several minutes before she picks her up. Sandra believes that babies can be spoiled if you go to them too quickly and hold them too much. She encourages Lexi to walk early and hopes that she'll be feeding herself by her first birthday. Sandra's own single mother instilled a strong sense in her four daughters that being independent and doing for themselves—not depending on others—was very important.

When 6-month-old Jordan cries, his dad, Alan, picks him up right away. As Jordan grows, Alan continues to rock him to sleep, rather than helping Jordan learn how to fall asleep on his own. When Alan sees Jordan struggling to make the Jack-in-the-Box pop up, he runs over to him quickly to turn the crank. Alan can't bear to see his son frustrated. He'd much rather step in, than allow Jordan to struggle with something on his own. Alan's own father always made him feel inadequate when he didn't get something right.

How did your mother, father, or other loved ones help you to feel good about yourself?

In what ways did they make you feel bad?

What do you do to help your child feel good about herself?

How did your mother or father comfort you when you were upset?

How do you comfort your child? When your parents were angry, what did they do?

How did that make you feel? How do you handle your anger with your child?

One of the things that most surprises new parents is the intense and shifting feelings.

Thinking about your reactions to your child enables you to reconsider your actions and make new choices. Sandra, for example, knows that her mother's insistence on self-reliance was a reaction to the fact that she was a single mom with little support in caring for four young girls. She taught her daughters the importance of being self-sufficient because she didn't want them to suffer and feel as helpless as she had. Sandra has enormous respect for her mother, but recognizes that her situation is different. Sandra has developed a support system for herself with friends and co-workers. She is learning that it's okay to rely on others and that nurturing Lexi won't keep her from growing up capable and strong. This kind of thinking frees Sandra to change her expectations to match Lexi's needs and abilities.

Alan, Jordan's dad, notices that Jordan gets frustrated easily. He also knows that his need to rescue Jordan from every struggle has more to do with his own childhood experiences than it does with Jordan's actual needs. Alan begins to question whether trying to do the opposite of what his own father did is really helping nurture Jordan's self-confidence, or whether it is in fact an obstacle. So he decides to try a new strategy. Rather than doing things for Jordan, Alan becomes his son's coach. Rather than solving problems for Jordan, Alan guides him as he struggles to solve problems for himself. This, he believes, may help Jordan feel competent to master challenges in a way Alan never did.

PARENTHOOD BRINGS LIFE CHANGES

Whatever changes you imagined that parenthood would bring, chances are you underestimated! One day you are responsible only for yourself. You can eat, sleep, and go to the bathroom whenever you like. No one is demanding your immediate attention.

With the birth of a child, every decision you make takes on new weight; from what and how you feed your baby, to whether or not you smoke, what kind of car you drive, what kind of clothing you wear, and where you live. Everything is considered from the perspective of how it will impact on this new life for which you are responsible. You feel like a grown-up in an entirely new way.

There will be times when your feelings seem overwhelming. As you gaze at your angelic, sleeping newborn, you may feel overcome with love and, at the same time, terrified about the awesome responsibility that lies before you. It's up to you to understand what your baby wants and needs, and how to muster the energy to meet those needs while taking care of yourself and all of your day-to-day responsibilities.

One of the things that most surprises new parents is the intense and shifting feelings. "One minute I am madly in love," said one new mom. "He looks at me with an ear-to-ear smile, and my heart melts. I feel so needed and important and loved. Then, half an hour later, he'll begin to cry, and nothing I can do will calm him. The crying seems endless. He seems to be really suffering, and I feel absolute panic. I feel useless. I feel like I'm not ready for this job, and the truth is, sometimes I feel angry at him for making me feel this way!"

All of these feelings are normal and can be intensified by the hormonal changes that moms experience, and the sleep deprivation that both moms and dads endure during the first few months. It's no wonder that so many new parents suffer from the "baby blues", a feeling of sadness that usually doesn't last more than a few weeks. If those blues persist, however, and interfere with your ability to take care of yourself or your baby, it's important to seek help from a trust-

My favorite part of parenting is…

My biggest challenge as a parent is…

I was least prepared for…

My biggest surprise was…

I worry most about…

Remember, taking care of yourself is one of the most important ways that you take care of your baby.

ed professional. Remember, taking care of yourself is one of the most important ways that you take care of your baby.

It also helps to remember that there is no right or wrong way to feel. What is important is that you recognize and accept your feelings for what they are, just feelings. This kind of acceptance enables you to think about what you're feeling and why you're feeling it, and that gives you more control over what you *do* with those feelings.

> Judy is a mom who's very uncomfortable with mess. When Ella, her 18-month-old, empties the contents of a cup on the table and starts finger painting with her juice, Judy feels her blood pressure rise. She wants to reach out and grab the cup, sponge up the mess, and remove Ella from the table. But she stops herself when she looks into her daughter's gleeful face. Judy wonders, what's more important, a clean table or Ella's experimentation?

By acknowledging her own need for order and cleanliness, Judy is able to stop herself from acting on an impulse to whisk away the cup and abruptly end her child's exploration. Instead, she comes up with a solution that meets her needs as well as her daughter's. She fills the bathtub in the middle of the day so that Ella can enjoy water play with cups and containers and lots of opportunities for filling, pouring, splashing, and exploring. "The bathtub is a good place to spill and splash," she tells her daughter. "The table is a good place to eat."

Nobody's Perfect

Parenting is a learning process, and as in all learning processes, you're bound to make mistakes. Every parent has ups and downs, and no parent gets it all "right." Fortunately, most children are quite flexible and bounce back quickly. The challenge for parents isn't to do things perfectly. Rather, it is to see your "mistakes" as opportunities to learn about yourself and your child. Over time, you'll discover what works and what doesn't.

James, a new dad, picks up his crying newborn, Danny, and begins to rock him gently as most parents would do. But the more James rocks, the more upset Danny seems to become. The more Danny cries, the more tense James feels. What's he going to do? He can't even calm his own son!

This scenario could play out in a number of ways. The more anxious and upset James becomes about his inability to calm Danny, the less likely it is that he'll succeed. Babies pick up on their parents' tension, and Danny is no exception. If, however, James can stop dumping on himself about his "personal failure," he will be able to see the situation as a learning opportunity. He might say to himself, "This isn't working for Danny; maybe I should try something else." Then, he might try different positions to see which one works best for Danny. He may discover that Danny doesn't like a lot of movement when he's upset. He may prefer to be held firmly against his dad's chest. Turning this situation into a learning opportunity will provide James with information that will be helpful for years to come.

What is the most difficult time of day?

How do you respond when you feel you've made a mistake?

What do you do best as a parent?

When do you need the most help?

Every parent has ups and downs, and no parent gets it all "right."

What do you find most stressful and frustrating about being a parent?

How do you cope?

Who are the people you can call for support?

KNOW AND RESPECT YOUR LIMITS

Parenting can be very stressful. Learning to recognize when you are about to reach your boiling point, and developing strategies to step away from your child before you boil over, is critical. This may mean putting an inconsolable child somewhere safe, like a crib, and taking a brief time-out.

All parents need support. The fact that we need support is not a sign of inadequacy. It just means that parenting is too hard a job for any one person to do alone all the time.

Deborah is having a bad day. She's home on maternity leave with her 2-month-old twins Jason and Jermaine, who seem to have little interest in sleeping. Deborah is exhausted. Meanwhile, there is a work emergency, and even though her colleagues said that they would handle everything themselves while she was gone, they have called her three times already today. To make matters worse, dishes and laundry are piling up, and her house is a mess. Deborah finds herself feeling annoyed and resentful at the over-whelming responsibility of taking care of two newborns and the rest of her life as well. She also sees that her being upset is clearly distressing the babies further, only adding to her stress. She knows that she needs to get some relief, but how?

Deborah then thinks of a woman she met at a support group for parents of multiples, who lives just a few blocks away, and wonders if she's home. Maybe if she can just get out of the house and talk with another adult, she'll feel better. She turns a blind eye to the messy house, loads the boys in the stroller, and sets off. Just getting out seems to calm both the boys and her; and luckily, her neighbor is home. By this time the babies are peacefully sleeping in their stroller, and Deborah enjoys coffee and commiseration with her new friend.

Knowing when to ask for support, and giving yourself permission to ask for it, doesn't come easily to many parents. It might mean asking a partner, or a friend or neighbor whom you trust to watch the baby while you take a well-deserved break. It might mean taking a walk to visit a friend, or getting a reliable and competent sitter or relative to come over and "share the care" during the late afternoon or early evening. Another option is calling or visiting a parent support center. The time during the day when you and your child are most cranky is the ideal time to schedule a break. And remind yourself that, in fact, babies benefit from building relationships with other people they can trust to care for them.

SHARING THE CARE OF YOUR CHILD

Sharing the care is essential for you and your child, but it isn't always easy. Allowing another person to be intimately involved with your child—whether it be a spouse, partner, relative, or child care provider—can evoke strong and sometimes uncomfortable feelings of jealousy, competition, blame, guilt, and even failure. Different people have different parenting styles, which are often based on their culture and childhood experiences; and it can be difficult to give up control over how your child is cared for.

Let's look at how a couple, Ross and Lauren, react differently to their son's frustration:

Ross has just presented his toddler, Thomas, with a new puzzle. Thomas gets to work with enthusiasm, but is soon screaming with frustration. He can't find the space for the bear. Lauren rushes in to see what the problem is, but Ross motions her away. He begins to coach Thomas. "You're right; the bear definitely doesn't fit there. How about another space?" he asks, pointing to open spaces on the board. Thomas tries another space, but that doesn't work either; and as his distress increases, so does his mom's. She is now giving Ross dirty looks, feeling that he's being too hard on Thomas. But Ross hangs in there. "Boy, this new puzzle is hard! It's going to take a lot of work! What about trying another space?" This time, Thomas finds the right

What do you and your partner agree on about raising children?

How do you differ?

What don't you like about how your partner or caregiver responds to your child?

How do you resolve your differences?

What do you feel that you can learn from each other's parenting style?

space and smiles with utter joy at his accomplishment. Lauren, who seconds ago was ready to take her husband to task, is surprised and delighted. She's learned something very important from him.

Fortunately, Lauren was able to keep her feelings in check while Ross worked things out with their son. No matter how upset she was, on some level she trusted her husband and the love he felt for their son. However, it isn't always easy to do that, especially when the disagreement is not with a loved one, but with a caregiver. Such differences can be about anything from how much a baby should sleep to a toddler's table manners, to when and how to begin toilet training.

Sometimes the issues are small and can be overlooked, especially if you feel confident that the caregiver is loving and responsible. For example, you may overlook the fact that grandma offers dessert after lunch, even though you generally don't like your child to have sweets.

At other times, however, when you feel very strongly about differences in styles, they need to be addressed—especially to ensure the health and safety of your child. When that's the case, communication is the key to resolving differences. You need to establish that you are all working together as a team to ensure the best care for your child. Listen with openness and respect, come up with a plan, try it out, and meet again to see how things are going. If necessary, adapt your plan.

When Denise first took her 5-month-old baby, Tyler, to a child care center, she was upset because the caregivers would let him lie on a blanket on the floor as long as he was content. Denise told the caregivers that she wanted them to hold Tyler more.

At first, his caregivers were annoyed. They felt that this mom had no understanding of the demands of working with a group of babies. But they kept the dialogue going. Denise explained that in her native country, babies were carried in a sling on their mother's back all day. She didn't want Tyler to be lonely. The caregivers, in turn, explained

Communication is the key to resolving differences.

how lying on the floor gave Tyler a chance to practice holding his head up, rolling over, reaching for toys, and playing with them. The caregivers explained that in a group setting, they couldn't carry Tyler around all of the time and still attend to all of the other children's needs, but they assured Denise that Tyler would always be held and comforted when he needed to be.

Denise and the caregivers came up with a plan: Denise would bring in a baby carrier so that the caregivers could carry Tyler around for some time each day. The caregivers would observe and tell Denise what kinds of things Tyler did when he was on the floor. At home, Denise would experiment with giving Tyler more time to play on the floor and see what happened. They would check back with each other in two weeks to see how things were going.

While sharing the care can be a challenge, it gives children an opportunity to learn new things about themselves and others...to broaden and enrich their lives and their understanding of the world around them.

While sharing the care can be a challenge, it gives children an opportunity to learn new things about themselves and others...to broaden and enrich their lives and their understanding of the world around them. These early experiences help children learn to build trusting and positive bonds with others, a lesson that will be useful throughout their lives.

TIME FOR YOURSELF AND IMPORTANT RELATIONSHIPS

Wendy, mom of 4-month-old Gina, misses going to the movies and seeing friends. She discusses this with her husband, Joe, and they agree that Sunday afternoons will be Wendy's time to do whatever she likes. After returning home from her first foray out, she finds Joe and Gina rolling around on the floor together in utter delight. Her fears about whether Gina would survive without her—would she take the bottle from Joe...would he be able to console her when she cried——were unfounded. Rather than feeling guilty as she suspected she might, Wendy feels new energy after her own excursion.

❖

Taking care of both your needs and the needs of your child is a difficult balancing act. Most parents are inclined to let their own needs slide as they attempt to do everything and be everything for their children. But the truth is that taking care of yourself—physically, emotionally, and spiritually—as well as the important relationships in your life—with your partner, friends, and family—is crucial for the

Do you take time for yourself?

What makes you feel cared for?

To do your best as a parent, what kind of help do you need from others?

What do you and your partner do to still have fun together?

What do you wish that you had more time for?

healthy development of your child. Why? For starters, because he grows up with a parent who models the importance of loving relationships. Beyond that, the important relationships in your life make you feel good. And when you feel good, you have more energy for your child, which makes him feel good about himself. So make time, as much as possible, to maintain your outside interests, whatever they may be—exercising, Thursday night ball games, reading, movies, having coffee with a friend.

As you keep in mind the special qualities that you bring to your relationship with your child, and what *you* need to be the best parent you can be, we now turn your attention to the other side of the equation—understanding who your child is and what makes him tick.

Taking care of both your needs and the needs of your child is a difficult balancing act.

2. Tuning In to *Your* *Child*

In Section 1 we explored how important it is to develop self-awareness. Of course, in addition to learning about who you are, you need to understand and appreciate who your child is. No two babies are alike, and chances are that your baby is every bit as complex as you are.

In the months leading up to a baby's birth, most parents have all kinds of ideas about what their child will be like. It's important to be aware of these images, so that you can put them aside and accept the child you have. Imagine, for example, if Michael Jordan's parents had been intent on his being a rock star, and Elvis Presley's parents had made up their minds that he would be a basketball legend!

Your child, like you, was born with a distinct personal style and approach to the world. One of the most important aspects of your job as a parent is to figure out just who your child is and to let her know that you value her. The better you understand what makes your child tick, the better you'll be able to nurture her talents. You can create an environment that fits your baby—an environment that will promote her development, build on her strengths, and provide the kind of support she needs to be all she can be. To do so, you need to take the time to tune in to what your baby is "telling" you.

The better you understand what makes your child tick, the better you'll be able to nurture her talents.

HOW DOES YOUR BABY LEARN ABOUT THE WORLD?

Your child learns about the world through his senses. The way he takes in stimulation through his senses and uses it to understand and interact with his world is known as sensory integration. For example, when a baby smells mom's milk, he knows that nourishment is coming and turns his mouth toward her.

For babies, the world is a banquet to be gobbled up with eyes, ears, nose, mouth, and fingers. Your baby might scan a room carefully with his eyes, focusing on details like the flowers on the wallpaper or the reflection of light off your eyeglasses. He notices all kinds of sounds, from the squeak of a door, to a tidbit of conversation. He reaches out to touch things; and as soon as he's able, he brings them to his mouth

For babies, the world is a banquet to be gobbled up with eyes, ears, nose, mouth, and fingers.

to explore with his lips and tongue. And he's passionate in his responses to new tastes. When something tastes good, you can't feed him fast enough, and when something tastes bad, he'll spit it out and shiver with disgust.

Although children use all of their senses as they explore the world around them, they may show a preference for one sense over another. One baby may love to use her eyes to explore, while another may seem more interested in new sounds. Children also vary in the amount of stimulation they can handle. Upon hearing a siren, one baby may show interest and excitement, another may cry in distress, and yet another may seem to ignore it altogether. The key is to offer lots of opportunities for your baby to explore with her senses and then watch to see what she likes best. This will help you learn what kind of "sensory diet," meaning the types and amount of stimulation, suits her.

Kara's parents noticed early on that she seemed especially sensitive to sounds—both pleasant and unpleasant. It would take Kara 15 minutes to recover from the blast of a car horn, but she always smiled and cooed when her parents played her favorite CD. On the other hand, Kara's cousin, Jack, barely noticed the sounds that delighted or terrified Kara. He was too absorbed by whatever was in his hand. He poked and waved and threw objects to the ground and screamed until someone picked them up so that he could start again. He was, his mom joked, "a hands-on kind of guy."

Kara's sensitivity to sound isn't better or worse than Jack's preference for touch—it's just different. And to the extent that parents and care-givers are aware of their baby's preferences and sensitivities, they can adapt to them. When parents begin thinking about how their child integrates sensory information at an early age, they can better support their child's lifelong development. Just remember to stay flexible and open to the possibility that a child who seems especially focused on mouthing or touching everything at one stage may become more visual later on.

WHAT IS YOUR CHILD'S PERSONAL STYLE?

A nother important way to learn about what makes your baby unique is to understand his personal style—his typical way of approaching the world—which is also known as temperament. You need only look at a room filled with toddlers to recognize the differences.

ADAPTABLE, CAUTIOUS, FEISTY

Consider the powerful impact of temperament as each of three toddlers—Alex, Charlie, and Frank—enters a new room in a child care center for the very first time. In one corner of the room is a group of tables with puzzles and art supplies. Another corner of the room is dominated by a climbing gym. A third corner has a large mirror with all kinds of dress-up paraphernalia hanging within a toddler's reach. In the center of the room is a block structure that is very much in use. Five toddlers are working together on constructing towers and roadways.

Alex and his mom open the door and scan the room. Within moments of entering, Alex rips off his coat and abandons his mom to join the children building with the blocks. He takes a block in his hand and sits down. "Make it big," one of the builders instructs Alex. "This big," Alex says, eagerly, reaching above his head.

Children like Alex are often described as *flexible, adaptable kids.* They generally approach new situations and new people easily. They have an easy time with transitions and are often described as kids who "go with the flow."

Charlie spends a long time leaning into his dad's leg and refuses to take off his coat or hat. He's watching. After a while, he inches away from his dad to get a closer look at a table where kids are working on puzzles. He returns to his dad's leg, but soon inches away again...this time toward the climbing gym. He lingers there for a while before pulling off his hat and bringing it to his dad to hold. At that point, Charlie's dad suggests that he remove his coat, and Charlie agrees. They walk together to a row of hooks and hang it up, and then Charlie takes his dad's hand, and they walk, together, back to the puzzle table. Charlie sits down next to another child and gets to work.

Kids like Charlie are usually *thoughtful* and *cautious*, especially on unfamiliar terrain. Sometimes, they can be fearful. They often have a difficult time with transitions and need lots of support and time to feel safe and comfortable.

Frank enters the room full speed ahead—no time to waste looking around to check out what's going on. He charges up to two boys nearby who are crawling on the floor, pushing fire trucks and making all kinds of siren sounds. He runs over to them, grabs one of the trucks, and yells, "MINE!"

Kids like Frank are often described as *feisty.* They are very passionate and intense and have difficulty controlling their strong feelings and desires. They jump for joy when happy and fume when they're not.

Most parents are attuned to their child's personal style. Alex's mom isn't surprised at Alex's ease. It never takes him long to dive in. Charlie's dad wasn't worried about his son eventually finding a comfortable place for himself in the room. He just wondered if it would take all day! Frank's mom knows that her son is very strong-willed. He knows what he wants and fights tooth and nail when anything gets in his way. She is sometimes a bit overwhelmed and embarrassed by Frank's intensity. At other times, she admires and is proud of it. The

Flexible, adaptable kids generally approach new situations and new people easily.

question is, once you have a clear sense of your child's temperament, what can you do to make life easier? Let's go back and look at Alex, Charlie, and Frank and see how their parents could best accommodate their personalities.

ADAPTING TO DIFFERENT TEMPERAMENTS

Most people assume that easygoing kids like Alex just sail through life without a worry in the world. In fact, no one ever just sails through life. Alex's parents can use his adaptable nature as a way to recognize when something is wrong. When a child who is generally very easygoing suddenly becomes clingy and more anxious, it can mean that something—either emotional or physical—is bothering him. Maybe he's brewing an ear infection. Maybe he's had too many recent changes in his life...a new sibling, a new house, *and* a new child care center. Maybe his mom is on a business trip, and he's worried that she won't come back. Young children don't always have the ability to explain what's bothering them, but when an easygoing guy like Alex undergoes a change in personality, it's time to do some detective work.

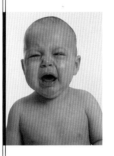

Children like Charlie, who enter new situations cautiously, generally require time and patience. You can help cautious children break the ice more easily, however, if you spend time preparing them for transitions, talking about what might happen, and communicating a strong sense of confidence that things will go well. If, for example, you smile and talk warmly to newcomers, your cautious child will get the message that the stranger is okay. It can also be helpful to let guests know, ahead of time, that it's best not to come on too strong. Often, it helps if the new person offers a child like Charlie an interesting object to explore to let him know he's a friend.

Intense and strong-willed children like Frank tend to feel out of control. Their emotions are so strong that they are often overwhelmed by them. As with a cautious child, feisty kids do best with lots of advance notice about what's happening next. Knowing what to expect helps them feel more in control, and their reactions may be less intense.

Intense and strong-willed children tend to get overwhelmed by their strong emotions.

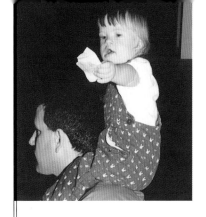

The fact that your child can surprise you is one of the most exciting and even delightful rewards of parenthood...if you let yourself go with the flow.

With older, feisty toddlers, you can help them gain some control over their reactions by talking, in advance, about how they might feel in an upcoming situation. If they are starting in a new classroom, you can talk about their excitement and their fears and then make a plan ahead of time for what they can do. For example, you might suggest that you first look around the room together and talk about what you see before jumping into the action. Getting his feelings out ahead of time helps him feel less overwhelmed later. And the more secure a child like Frank feels, the less need he'll have to gain control in unacceptable ways, such as shouting, hitting, or grabbing.

TEMPERAMENT TRAITS

As you spend time watching your baby, you'll begin to notice patterns in her behavior that will allow you to anticipate her needs, keep her secure and comfortable, and provide experiences that will promote both learning and the development of healthy relationships. Remember: There is no right or wrong way for a baby to be. What's most important is that you understand and adapt to your child's style so that you can help her adapt to the world.

It's also important to keep track of who you are, how you and your child are similar, and how you are different. Two people who are very different can have a very close relationship and even introduce each other to new experiences that they might not have had with someone similar to them. But for the relationship to work, differences must be respected.

Finally, keep in mind that children are not predictable. Sometimes they surprise you by acting in ways that are not typical. A child who is usually wary of strangers might fall madly in love with someone he's never seen before...and you won't have a clue as to why. The fact that your child can surprise you is one of the most exciting and even delightful rewards of parenthood...if you let yourself go with the flow.

FIVE SPECIFIC TRAITS

Your child's style gives you important information about why he behaves and reacts the way he does. In order to help you put together a picture of your "whole child"—whether he is more adaptable, cautious, or feisty—researchers who study infant temperament have identified specific traits that help describe a child's individual way of approaching the world. These include:

• HOW INTENSELY THE CHILD RESPONDS TO THINGS

• HOW ACTIVE THE CHILD IS

• HOW THE CHILD INTERACTS WITH OTHERS

• HOW THE CHILD RESPONDS TO CHANGE

• HOW PERSISTENT OR EASILY FRUSTRATED THE CHILD IS

Each of the following five sections explores a specific temperament trait that will help you identify your child's personal style.

INTENSITY OF REACTION:
BIG REACTORS, LOW REACTORS

Feisty Frank tells the world how he feels in a voice that's loud and clear. He's what we call a Big Reactor. Big Reactors express supreme happiness by squealing with delight and can express anger by shouting, throwing things, hitting, and biting. Their reactions to physical stimuli are every bit as intense as their reactions to emotional stimuli. A Big Reactor may not be able to tolerate an itchy tag on a T-shirt, or the wrinkle in a sock, or an unpleasant smell. A trip to the barber with a Big Reactor can be a nightmare.

At the other end of the spectrum are children we'll call Low Reactors. Parents of Low Reactors often feel blessed during their infancy because they seem less demanding than other babies. They're quiet, rarely fuss, and tend to sleep a lot. The fact that these babies are so undemanding, however, doesn't necessarily mean that they require less effort on the part of parents. On the contrary, you may have to work harder to attract and hold their attention.

For many children, intensity isn't an issue at all. Their reactions fall somewhere between Low and Big Reactors, and they tend to take things in stride. Their moods are fairly even. They smile when they're happy and complain, in a reasonable way, when they're not.

What is my child's favorite way to be held, touched, and talked to?

How does my baby react to new situations?

How does he react to a sudden noise?

How does my baby show me that she feels good, angry, or sad?

Are my child and I similar or different with regard to the intensity of our reactions?

- **Talk to her about who she is.** "You're an on-the-go girl!"

- **Remember: Active babies aren't wild or out of control.** They just need to move.

How you might respond to a Sitter:

- **Respect her pace and style.** Offer her lots of opportunity to play with the things that she enjoys, such as books, dress up clothes, puzzles, building blocks, toy figures, etc. (And remember, you still need to babyproof, even if she's not moving around a lot!)

- **Let her look before she leaps.** If she prefers watching kids on the climbing gym, let her watch. Then suggest trying something together...like going down the slide on your lap. But always remember to follow her lead and take it slow.

- **Play hide-and-seek.** When one of you is found, entice her into a chasing game.

- **Listen to music together.** It's easy to shift from listening to dancing...if the music moves you!

- **Remember: There's nothing wrong with being a "sitter."** As long as she gets the exercise she needs and can enjoy a range of activities, she can be happy and healthy.

Some babies are content to sit quietly in one place and travel around with their eyes.

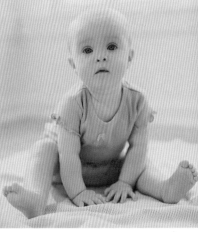

INTERACTION WITH OTHERS:
FROM "GLAD TO MEET YOU" TO "LET'S TAKE IT SLOW" KIDS

How does my child typically react when meeting someone new?

Is my child more comfortable with adults or with other children?

How does my child react to a new group of kids? Of adults?

Are my child and I similar or dissimilar in this regard?

Do those similarities or differences make me uncomfortable?

Some children approach new people—both adults and other children—in a very eager and inviting way. They project a sense of openness and ease when they encounter a new face that everyone picks up on and responds to. Baby Ricky immediately hands her mom's new friend a book and settles into her lap. Eighteen-month-old Ben takes a new classmate by the hand, escorts him to the art table, and offers paper and crayons. And 2 1/2-year-old Laura strokes her new child care provider's bracelet, gazes up at her, and says, "Pretty." Even before they could talk, these children engaged newcomers by smiling, cooing, and looking them in the eye. The more the merrier, they seem to say, as they make their entrance and work the room!

Other children are more hesitant and shy around people they don't know. They need time to warm up before they feel comfortable enough to interact. They may also be quite happy to play on their own, or with just one familiar friend or adult. And they're always eager to hang out with you. They don't necessarily need a lot of friends to be happy. In fact, they're likely to be just as content as more social children.

Most children fall somewhere in the middle. Sometimes they're hesitant and need some help and support around new people, and sometimes they jump right in.

HOW YOU MIGHT RESPOND TO A "GLAD TO MEET YOU" KID:

♦ **Provide lots of opportunity for social interaction.** He thrives on it.

♦ **Validate how much he likes being with others.** Give him time to play on his own as well, so he learns that he can also be content by himself—that he doesn't always need to be playing with someone to be happy.

HOW YOU MIGHT RESPOND TO A "LET'S TAKE IT SLOW" KID:

• **Think of yourself as a safe, home base.** Introduce him to new people from the safety of your arms. Place him on your lap near another child and talk about what the other child is doing in a soothing, reassuring voice.

• **Communicate positive feelings toward others non-verbally.** Use your facial expressions and body language. Your child looks to you for cues.

• **Suggest that new people take it slow when they interact with your child.** Give them your child's favorite toy or book, and let them use it as a bridge to connect with him.

• **Whenever possible, prepare your child to meet new people ahead of time, and give him lots of time to get used to places—such as a new child care center—before you leave him.** "We're going to a new friend's house together. They have a dog..." The more he knows ahead of time, the more comfortable he'll feel.

• **Remember: There's nothing wrong with being a "Let's Take It Slow" kid.** Like adults, children have different needs for social interaction to feel content and connected.

COPING WITH CHANGE:
FROM "LET'S GO" TO "LET'S STAY HERE" KIDS

How does my child react to a change in routine?

Does my baby enjoy new foods or prefer the same-old-same-old?

How easy is it for me to shift my child from one activity to the next—bath to bed, park to home, play to dinner?

Are my child and I similar or dissimilar in this regard?

Some children, like Adaptable Alex, take change in stride. For them, new jackets, new friends, new foods, and new babysitters all seem to make life more interesting. When they are very young, they're the kind of babies you can take anywhere. They'll nap in a noisy restaurant and nurse wherever you happen to be.

Other kids, like Feisty Frank, are much more sensitive to change. Their hairs stand on end in response to even the smallest of shifts—a new nipple on the bottle, a new food on their plate, or the tiniest change in a regular routine. As toddlers, these children show their distress by throwing tantrums. A tantrum might be triggered by the suggestion of a new babysitter or a change of furniture in their house. Ultimately, these children manage to make the necessary adjustments, but they need lots of time and support to get comfortable in new surroundings or with new people. And before they make their adjustments, you can expect lots of "No, No, No!"

Most children fall somewhere in the middle. They may have an easy time with new foods, but a more difficult time with new people. They may be cautious around unknown adults, but jump right in when it comes to their peers. Given some time to get used to a change or new situation, they feel safe, at ease, eager to explore.

HOW YOU MIGHT RESPOND TO A "LET'S GO" KID:

- **Be sensitive to her signals.** When a child is extremely easygoing, we can sometimes take for granted that any change is okay.

- **Let her know about new situations ahead of time.** For example, tell her in advance when she's going to a new place, or meeting someone new. Kids who enjoy new situations also enjoy talking about them and anticipating them.

HOW YOU MIGHT RESPOND TO A "LET'S STAY HERE" KID:

- **Establish routines.** Create a predictable plan for transitional times (mornings, bedtimes, hellos and good-byes, etc.) and stick to it as much as possible

- **Make sure that she gets plenty of rest.** Fatigue makes it even more difficult to cope with change.

- **Ease into new activities.** Talk about them first, and arrive early enough to get comfortable.

- **Offer advance notice when an activity is about to end.** "When this book is finished, we're going home." "When the timer rings, it's time for bath."

- **Use familiar objects to ease anxiety during transitions.** A new doctor will be less scary if your child has her favorite blanket in hand.

- **Offer realistic choices as she gets older.** Give her a sense of control about how she wants to make transitions. "Would you like to sing one more song before we leave?"

PERSISTENCE, PATIENCE, AND FRUSTRATION:
"LET'S TRY AGAIN" VERSUS "I'M DONE" KIDS

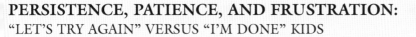

Persistence means not giving up when faced with a challenge. It is the ability to stick with a difficult task and cope with frustration. Think about Karla and Abby—two children building block towers. Karla gets the tower waist-high before it tumbles. She pauses, looks at the blocks on the floor, and begins again. This time she gets the tower shoulder high. When it tumbles, she gets to work on her third tower. This time she builds it all the way to the top of her head. She looks at her work approvingly and calls her mom in for a special viewing. When Mom says, "I'll be there in a few minutes, as soon as I finish what I'm doing," Karla busies herself with another game and waits. Karla is both persistent and patient. The two traits usually go hand in hand.

Abby starts to cry when her waist-high tower tumbles. She manages, through tears, to start again, but this time it falls with the fourth block. She stamps her foot, picks up a block, throws it against the wall, and cries for her mom. When her mom says that she'll be right there, Abby dissolves into tears and begins screaming for her, "Mommy, mommy, mommy!" When mom comes running in and suggests moving on to another activity, there's little she can do to

How does my child react when he doesn't get what he wants?

When my child has a hard time doing something, does he keep trying, simply stop, or have a tantrum?

Am I more or less persistent than my child? How do I cope with frustrations, disappointments, and challenges?

How patient am I as a parent?

comfort her. Abby is a child with a low frustration level and little patience. Those two traits usually go hand in hand as well.

How you might respond to a "Let's Try Again" kid:

♦ **Join her in her play**. It's easy to let her play alone for long periods because she is less likely to demand your presence. But she needs and benefits from your interaction together, even if she doesn't need much help.

♦ **As she grows, let her know that everyone needs help sometimes and that you are available.** Sometimes children get so much positive feedback for being independent that it's hard for them to ask for help when they do need it.

How you might respond to an "I'm done" kid:

♦ **If your child has to wait for something (food, attention, etc.), talk to her about what you are doing.** "I'm taking your food out of the fridge." "Daddy is taking his coat off and coming to give you a big hug."

♦ **When she falls apart, let her know that you appreciate how hard it can be.** "Puzzles are hard! It makes you so mad when the bear won't fit in the space." Then become her coach. Help her think through solutions without doing the work for her. Suggest or demonstrate strategies, like trying another space for the bear.

♦ **Teach her to pace herself when frustration is building.** Offer time away from the frustrating task for a hug or a cozy snuggle with a book. Then return to the challenge with new energy.

♦ **Maintain your sense of humor.** Children will appreciate it if, for example, you yell at the block that has fallen: "You silly block! You just won't stay up there!...Well you can't beat us; we're not giving up if it takes us all day!"

♦ **Remember: Some children take longer to develop patience and persistence.** It just takes time and patience on the part of mom, dad, and caregivers.

Putting It All Together

We began this section by talking about how important it is to understand who your child is so that you can be sensitive and responsive to his needs and nurture his talents. We talked about sensory integration and temperament—all pieces of a puzzle that come together to create a true and meaningful picture of your child.

Now, put this together with what you discovered in Section 1 when you explored your own identity both as an individual and as a parent. Think about that picture of yourself. How is it similar to or different from the picture of your child? Do they fit together well? Are there clashes?

Again, there is no right or wrong way to parent. The goal is to take two pictures, which may be more or less similar, and find the best way for them to work together.

This final story, about a 2-year-old named Sam, and his dad, Mark, shows how you can use your insights into yourself and your child to help guide you to sensitively (and as accurately as possible!) understand and respond to your child's individual needs. While this takes time and patience and can feel quite challenging at times, it will help you create a relationship that brings both of you satisfaction and joy.

> Mark is eager to explore a new playground with Sam, but his enthusiasm is soon replaced by disappointment when he realizes that Sam seems overwhelmed by the scene. There are lots of kids running around in every direction, and the noise is ear-piercing. Mark tries to entice Sam to a quieter area, but Sam won't let go of his dad's leg; Sam's other hand tightly grasps his favorite bear. Mark has an impulse to just pick Sam up and place him on the slide, but he stops to think about what's really going on and tries to figure out the best way to proceed. What is Sam trying to tell him? And why does he find Sam's behavior so upsetting?

What's important is that you hang in there. Don't give up or spend too much time blaming yourself.

As Mark sits on the bench, with Sam on his lap, he thinks about himself and his son. He realizes that he wants Sam to be assertive and athletic because those are qualities he has always valued in himself. At the same time, he recognizes that Sam is generally happier and more relaxed in one-on-one situations and that he's always needed time to adjust to new places, experiences, and people. Mark also remembers how *he* felt as a boy, when his dad would often say things like, "Look at Johnny—*he* can do it," leaving Mark with the sense that he never quite measured up. Mark decides that pushing Sam won't make him less afraid. It will only make him feel badly about himself and less trusting. Mark wants to help Sam feel competent about his abilities and self-confident enough to try new challenges. So he continues to sit quietly with Sam on a park bench and gives him a hug. He feels his son's arms around his neck and gets a pang. Sam is a wonderful, loving, thoughtful little boy who needs to be valued and accepted for who he is—not changed into someone Mark wants him to be.

After a while, Mark points out the kids playing hide-and-seek and the toddler struggling to climb the stairs to the slide. Sam climbs off Mark's lap and stands on the pavement, between his dad's knees. Sam begins to relax and is soon pointing at the kids and laughing. He takes Mark's hand, and they walk around the playground, giggling as they send Sam's beloved bear down the slide. Mark gets on the swing and suggests that Sam push him, an idea that Sam finds wildly funny. Then he invites Sam to sit on his lap while he swings. Mark snuggles him tight and begins to sing, which always makes Sam happy. Soon Mark is helping Sam and another toddler make a cake together in the sandbox. When it's time to leave, Sam begs to stay longer, and Mark feels gratified. He had a great afternoon with his son...with his *real* son, not the child of his imagination, but a much more interesting, thoughtful, and delightful little boy.

While you won't always feel up to taking the time or energy to think about every interaction with your child in this in-depth way, the good news is that you will get lots of opportunities to do so. All parents do things they regret; and by and large, no single "mistake" does irreversible damage. What's important is that you hang in there. Don't give up or spend too much time blaming yourself. Give yourself 5 minutes to wallow in your guilt and then use your energy constructively. Think about what went wrong and what you might do differently next time. Your child will give you many chances to try again.

Now that you have a clear sense of who you are and who your child is, we conclude in Section 3 by looking at general development in the first 3 years of life. A detailed chart is provided to help guide you in reading and responding to typical behaviors that you might see, based on what you now know about your child's unique attributes.

Forcing children to do something they're not ready for can make them more afraid and insecure about trying new things.

3. The Amazing First Three Years of *Life*

The first 3 years of a child's life are a time of incredible development. If you stop to think about what's actually happening in a very compressed amount of time—3 years, after all, is just a tiny segment of our lives—it's quite remarkable. Just place a newborn next to a 3-year-old and consider the differences between the two.

By the time children are 3, they have learned to dress and feed themselves, to walk, to dance, to talk, to sing, to imagine, to give and accept love, to be confident and secure, to show empathy, to be curious, and much, much more. The development that occurs during those first 3 years lays the foundation for a lifetime of learning.

While babies are learning at a fast pace during this time of life, they all learn at different rates. We've already talked about the fact that babies are born with different ways of learning about the world through their senses and different temperaments and that these attributes affect the way they learn. Consider two babies presented with a Jack-in-the-Box. A baby who loves to move may be so busy crawling and climbing that he doesn't spend much time working on the fine motor (finger) skills necessary to get the Jack-in-the Box to pop up. On the other hand, a baby who loves to explore with his hands can make "Jack" appear long before he focuses his energy on crawling.

Another important factor to keep in mind, as you think about your child's development, is that each area of development—intellectual, social, emotional, motor, and language—depends on and influences other areas. Consider the 9-month-old who reaches her arms up to tell her dad that she "wants up." This apparently simple gesture is, in fact, very complex. It begins with the baby's desire to be picked up and held. This feeling is an indication of her emotional development. The fact that she doesn't want to be picked up by just anyone, only her dad, shows that she has developed a close and trusting relationship with him and is a signpost of her social development. Her intellectual development is reflected by that fact that she has figured out a way to communicate her desires: If I "lift up my arms, he'll know that I want him to pick me up." Finally, she has to have the physical coordination—the motor development—to be able to stretch her arms up in the right direction and send her message.

The development that occurs during those first 3 years lays the foundation for a lifetime of learning.

Your sensitive, responsive caregiving and interactions with your baby are more important to her development than any toy.

EAGER LEARNERS

From day one, babies are ready and eager to learn. No one has to tell babies to practice crawling, or babbling, or filling up and dumping out. They are driven to practice new skills by something deep inside. They want to master challenges. They are delighted to display their competence. They light up our lives with their pride.

Just because our babies are so motivated to learn, however, doesn't mean that they don't need us. In fact, we can model for our children how to take the next step to build on their learning. For example, if your toddler is playing with his favorite stuffed bear, you can offer the bear a drink, helping to build your child's imagination. As long as we respect the fact that each child develops at his or her own pace, there is a lot we can do to encourage their development.

BABIES AND THE BRAIN

Thanks to new technology, brain researchers can see just how complex and active a young child's brain is. We now know, for example, that a range of early experiences affect how the brain is actually wired. Those parts of your baby's brain concerned with language are being shaped long before she utters her first word, as she listens to you coo and talk. Parts of the brain that will eventually enable her to walk are being fired up when, as a newborn, she waves her arms and legs randomly in the air. All of this happens without the need for "educational" toys or structured activities "guaranteed" to make your baby "smarter." What you are already doing in your everyday activities and interactions with your child are all the "brain exercises" she needs.

You help your baby's healthy brain development when you respond sensitively to what your baby is "telling" you with her sounds, facial expressions, and body gestures. For example, babies can sometimes get overloaded. When your baby turns her eyes or body away, arches her back, or even hiccups, she may be telling you that she needs a break. This could mean a break from playing, from specific sights or sounds, or maybe from too many people around her. When you sensitively read and respond to her signals, for example, by lowering your voice, stopping a game, or turning down the music, you will help your baby to relax and feel content. This then helps her focus her attention on her most important job—learning about the world around her. Your sensitive, responsive caregiving and interactions with your baby are more important to her development than any toy.

READING YOUR BABY'S SIGNALS

It takes patience and practice to learn how to read your baby's signals. You won't understand everything, but if you keep working at it, you'll understand enough to promote his healthy development. Through an ongoing process of trial and error, combined with your own instincts and intuition, you'll find the best way to respond.

The following chart will help you figure out your baby's signals. It identifies typical behaviors that you might observe at different stages in your child's early development, offers possible explanations of what he may be trying to communicate, and makes suggestions for how you might respond. You can adapt these responses, based on what you know about your child's temperament.

As you study the chart, you'll notice that we've kept age ranges for developmental milestones very broad. We've done this intentionally, because the more we learn about babies, the clearer it is that no two babies develop at the same rate. Development is not a race. It unfolds in stages that can span several months, and whether a baby reaches a milestone earlier or later within the normal time frame isn't significant.

Birth to 8 Months: Your Remarkable Baby

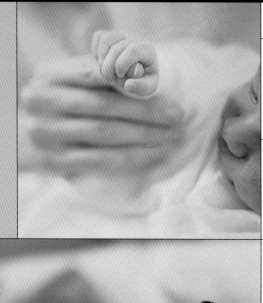

...stops crying because she sees you coming.

...cries, coos, gurgles, whimpers, smiles, rubs his eyes, arches his back, turns his head away, opens his eyes widely.

...startles and cries at loud noises.

...breaks into tears when you arrive to pick him up from child care.

...smiles and responds with pleasure when you talk, sing, or read to her.

...cries or clings to you when a new person approaches.

...observes his own hands; pulls off your glasses; sticks his fingers in your nose; reaches for a toy; grabs the phone.

...holds up her head; turns from stomach to back and from back to stomach; creeps forward or backward; crawls; makes other strides in gross motor development.

YOUR CHILD MIGHT BE SAYING:	WHAT YOU CAN DO:
I know I can count on you when I have a problem. I trust your love. Don't worry about spoiling me. When I get what I need when I need it, I feel good about myself and the people around me.	◆ Respond promptly when she cries. ◆ Look for patterns in her cries and other cues. Is she tired? Wet? Hungry? Bored? Lonely?
Watch me carefully! I communicate through cries, facial expressions, and movements when I'm sleepy, hungry, wet, frightened, bored, overwhelmed, or interested.	◆ Trust your instincts when you respond to your baby. His response will tell you if you're on target. If not, try something else.
I'm sensitive to sounds. Some kids might love loud cars and trucks, but not me. I learn that it's safe to show you how I feel because you comfort me when I'm distressed.	◆ Acknowledge feelings and offer reassurance: "That fire engine scared you, but you're safe." ◆ Introduce her slowly, in the safety of your arms, to new sounds and places.
When I see you after a long day, I remember how much I've missed you. I save my most intense feelings for you because I trust you. You always come back.	◆ Don't rush out. Join him in finishing what he was doing when you arrived to get him. ◆ Establish a "going home" ritual. Rituals are a comforting way to ease transitions.
I love it when we share words and songs. When I see how much fun words can be, it makes me want to keep "talking" and learning.	◆ Spend lots of time reading together. Let her choose the books. ◆ Narrate what you do together.
I don't know this person. I don't know what to expect from her, and that scares me.	◆ Give your child the space and time—in your arms or on your lap—to get used to new people. ◆ Urge others to approach slowly. Have them break the ice by offering an interesting object.
I am learning about how the world works and all of the things I can do with my own hands. I'm pretty amazing!	◆ Encourage his curiosity by offering safe objects to explore. ◆ Guide his hands gently as he explores your face. ◆ Share his excitement about new discoveries.
I am learning how to make my body do what I want it to do. I'm so thrilled with what I can do that, sometimes, I just can't seem to stop. I want to practice all of the time!	◆ Provide lots of opportunities for her to explore with her body, such as creeping to get an object. ◆ Babyproof your home so that she can move safely and that you don't spend all of your time saying, "No."

WHEN YOUR CHILD...

...looks up at you and smiles when she has done something great.

...grabs for the spoon while you feed her or smears cooked carrot all over her face, high-chair tray, and you.

...protests at bedtime.

...clings or cries when you are leaving.

...makes marks with crayons, stacks blocks, uses a spoon, drinks from a cup, and does other things to show off her small motor development.

...responds to music by dancing, moving, and brightening up.

...toddles over after venturing off on his own and grabs your legs.

...points to something and then looks over to share her discovery with you.

YOUR CHILD MIGHT BE SAYING:	WHAT YOU CAN DO:
Look at me! Look at me! I'm awesome! When I know that you're proud, too, it makes me eager to try new things.	◆ Share her pleasure in her accomplishments. ◆ Create opportunities for her to master new skills.
I want to feed myself. The more things I do for myself, the better I feel!	◆ Offer safe finger foods and a child's spoon to hold and practice using as you feed her. ◆ Forget about mess! Use big bibs, bathe her after dinner, and put a rubber mat under the highchair.
There are too many exciting things going on for me to go to sleep. I want to be with you.	◆ Tell him when bedtime is approaching. ◆ Establish a regular bedtime routine: bath, bed, book...or whatever works. ◆ Offer him a sense of control; let him pick the book or song.
I love you. You make me feel safe. I can't bear the idea of your leaving because I need you for so many things.	◆ Remind yourself that separations are difficult. ◆ Play games like peekaboo to prepare him for separation. ◆ When you say, "good-bye", calmly reassure him that you always come back.
I am learning to use my hands to explore and do things for myself. I'm so proud of what I can do! It keeps me occupied and helps me learn about all kinds of new things.	◆ Offer objects that give her a chance to practice using her fingers such as spoons, cups and safe, but small toys. ◆ Teach her how meaningful her activities are. Send her scribbles in a letter to grandma. Have her help with cleaning up, now that she's able.
This sounds great! I love to move, move, move!	◆ Join in, laugh, dance, have a great time. ◆ Keep the music playing.
No matter where I go, you'll always be there for me. You're my home base. As I venture off, I know I can always return to you.	◆ Greet your returning traveler with a big hug that lets him know you love him. ◆ Play peekaboo or hide-and-seek, great games that will help him cope with separations.
Look at what I discovered. I want to see it or smell it or hold it. Can you get it for me so I can touch it, smell it, taste it?	◆ Talk about her discoveries and lift her to see, smell, or touch them. ◆ If it's safe, offer her the object to explore.

WHEN YOUR CHILD...

...says, "No!" and starts challenging rules and pushing limits.

...sometimes acts like he's going on 15 and other times acts like a baby again.

...has trouble knowing when to stop.

...hits, pushes, or bites another child.

...has a temper tantrum.

...plays pretend games with stuffed animals or make-believe toys like telephones, stoves, cars or dress up clothes.

Competent Toddler

YOUR CHILD MIGHT BE SAYING:	WHAT YOU CAN DO:
I am a person with my own ideas. I am learning who I am and how to behave by trying out different ways and seeing which works best.	◆ Encourage independence with limited choices: "Red or blue sweater?" not "Which sweater?" ◆ Establish consistent limits. ◆ Maintain a sense of humor, and don't become rigid.
I want to be grown-up and independent, but sometimes I get scared and need to know you're there for me. Try to be patient. This isn't easy for me either!	◆ Be flexible. Support his independence, but let him revisit babyhood. ◆ Let him help with real work, like table setting, so that he can feel "big." ◆ Maintain special rituals from babyhood, for example, a bedtime routine.
I can't always put the brakes on when I'm having a great time. Sometimes the things I'm doing are so-o-o exciting! With your help I'll learn about self-control, but don't expect it to happen overnight.	◆ Establish clear rules and stick to them: "Balls are for outside." "All food and drinks at the table." Expect that he'll need reminders. ◆ Always acknowledge when he shows self-control: "You remembered to bring your milk to the table. Good job!"
I'm angry, frustrated, or maybe just overexcited. I can't control myself. Help me, please!	◆ Watch for rising tension and signs of potential conflict. Step in before things get out of control. ◆ Acknowledge feelings: "You're angry that Jake took your cookie." ◆ Be clear about acceptable behavior: "It's okay to be angry, but it's not okay to hit."
I've lost control. Maybe it's because I'm frustrated, tired, or angry. Or maybe I'm just overwhelmed by too much going on around me, and I need a break.	◆ Look for patterns to figure out what triggers his tantrums. ◆ When it's over, put his feelings into words, and make a plan for next time: "You got frustrated putting your shoe on. Next time you can ask for help."
I'm practicing being a grown-up by doing things just like you. In my imagination, I can do anything and be anyone. That's the best part of play.	◆ Encourage imaginary play by providing lots of props and joining in. "I'm hungry. Make me a snack please." ◆ Follow her lead and don't take over. You're a visitor in her world—she knows the rules!

As your toddler grows, let him do more for himself. Put a stool near the sink so he can brush his teeth. Let him select his clothing and help sort laundry. It all builds self-esteem.

WHEN YOUR CHILD...

...wants to play more and more with other children.

...has trouble sharing or taking turns.

...throws a ball, stands on one foot, walks up the stairs, eats with a spoon and fork, pours milk on her cereal and pulls on her own shirt and pants.

...tells you when his diaper is wet, or runs to the potty and sits on it fully clothed.

...gets frustrated trying to express herself.

...wants you to read the same stories over and over.

Competent Toddler (cont'd)

YOUR CHILD MIGHT BE SAYING:	WHAT YOU CAN DO:
I'm not the same as you. You're a big person, and I like to play with little people who look and act like me. I learn by watching what they do; and when I play with them, they become my special friends. I love having friends.	◆ Provide lots of opportunities for interaction with peers. ◆ Know your child and what her ideal play situation is, for example: how long before she gets tired, how many friends to play with at once, what the best time of day is for playdates.
I'm beginning to learn that things aren't always the way I want them to be. It will take me a while and lots of practice to develop these skills.	◆ Let older toddlers try to work things out for themselves before stepping in to help. ◆ Introduce the idea of turn-taking, but don't expect much. Toddlers are too young to master it.
I'm getting to be very grown up. I can do so many things for myself every day now. Sometimes I don't want any help from you. But I never mind hearing how terrific you think I am.	◆ As your toddler grows, let him do more for himself. Put a stool near the sink so he can brush his teeth. Let him select his clothing and help sort laundry. It all builds self-esteem.
I know just what's happening in my body and I'm thinking about starting to use this potty.	◆ Follow his lead. Forcing can lead to resistance and power struggles. ◆ Expect lots of interest in potty activities, including company whenever you go to the bathroom. ◆ Expect accidents and never punish for them. Treat them matter-of-factly.
I can't always figure out how to say what I mean. Sometimes I stumble on my words because I can't get them out as fast as I want.	◆ Acknowledge her frustration. ◆ Be patient and listen carefully. ◆ Offer words for what she may be trying to say: "Are you sad you dropped your ice-pop?"
This story is like an old friend. It makes me feel safe and secure. I like knowing what to expect, and I love knowing what all the words mean. Pretty soon I'll tell you the story and you can listen.	◆ Honor her requests when she asks for a story. ◆ Leave out the last word of a sentence and see if she fills it in. ◆ Change a word and see if she corrects you. ◆ When you just can't bear reading that same book again, ask her to "read" it to you or to a special doll.

4. Thoughts to *Grow On*